GW00359687

The good behaviour guide

The essential handbook for dog owners
by David Appleby MSc CCAB
Founder Member of the Association of Pet Behaviour Counsellors

Published in the United Kingdom by
The Pet Behaviour Centre
Upper Street, Defford, Worcestershire WR8 9AB, UK

© 1990, 2002, 2004 David Appleby
David Appleby has asserted his right
under the Copyright, Designs and Patents Act, 1988
to be identified as the author of this work.
Illustrations by Sarah Thompson and Jean-Claude Delord

First edition published in the UK 1990, second edition in 2002
and third edition in 2004

ISBN 0-9546595-1-1

Anyone who owns a dog as a companion knows what a joy they can be. When we see dogs on film, Police or Guide Dogs working, it is difficult to believe that a well loved and cared for dog could ever be a problem. However, if you ask your family and friends you are almost certain to hear of someone who has had real difficulties or even worse, had to part with a dog because they could not cope. This sad state of affairs can be avoided if the right things are done.

Why do things go wrong?

Mainly because we fail to guard against disaster. Most dogs are perfectly well behaved despite the approach and attitude their owners adopt, not because of it. In other words you can do all the wrong things and get away with it, but this is not very responsible and unfortunately if things do go wrong, it is the dog that quite unjustifiably gets the blame. We must look upon doing the 'right' thing as insurance against problems developing instead of reacting when they occur. This booklet is designed to help you prevent problems or to start the process of resolving them if they have occurred.

Throughout the booklet dogs and puppies are referred to as 'he'. This is for convenience only and all advice is equally applicable to females.

WHAT ARE THE MAIN PROBLEMS THAT CAN BE PREVENTED OR IMPROVED IF WE DO THE RIGHT THINGS?

Fearful behaviour

Problems related to puppy development:
   Chewing
   Inappropriate toileting
   Play biting

Boisterousness & general lack of control

Separation problems due to over-attachment (separation anxiety) which can result in symptoms that include:
   Destructive behaviour
   Vocal behaviour
   Loss of toilet control

Aggression:
   Aggression related to resources towards family members
   Territorial aggression towards visitors
   Fear/apprehension towards individuals who un-nerve the dog
   Aggression between dogs in the same household

FEARFUL BEHAVIOUR

How can we help prevent fearful behaviour?

The first few weeks of a puppy's life are crucial in the development of behavioural organisation and confidence. Breeders start the development of sound temperament by selecting the right parents and rearing the puppies in the house where they can receive more experience than they would in a barn, shed, or kennel. After six weeks of age, new owners should continue the process in their own environment.

What is behavioural organisation?

Behavioural organisation describes the process whereby puppies become familiar with their environment and the animals they will interact with when older e.g., people, other dogs, cats, and learn how to respond to them. Experience is important and particularly so during between three and five weeks of age when puppies are in a natural state of relaxation, manifested by a low heart rate. Consequently, the things they meet are likely to be associated with a relaxed emotional state. For example the breeder should ensure that it meets as many people from both genders and all age groups as possible. Of course the process is ongoing and you must carry it on once you have obtained your puppy so that it has the best chance of learning to be confident in the world at large.

In pack society, this is also the period in which a puppy learns social rules, its position within the group and to cope with the frustration that comes with not getting what it wants when it wants it. Its mother, littermates, and other group members all contribute to this learning and families must continue the process to give their puppy the best chance of living with them harmoniously throughout its lifetime. (See 'Aggression related to resources' page 13).

Helpful Tip: *Daily examination of your puppy's teeth, ears, paws, and the area around his tail will condition him to accept this form of contact. It will help prevent fearful behaviour when examined by your veterinary surgeon, and first aid will be easier to achieve.*

Exposure to other dogs does not imply allowing a puppy to run amuck with them, especially if those dogs have poor communication skills. If allowed to happen, problems triggered by the presence of other dogs, such as reduced control, poor canine communication skills, and frustration-related aggression could develop. Special classes are available where puppies socialise with each other, a range of people and learn control. You must start as soon as all vaccinations are completed to gain the full benefit. Your veterinary practice should be able to advise you about classes in your locality. They may also run puppy parties, which will help to achieve these objectives and develop positive associations with the veterinary environment.

What about the environment?

Exposure to a range of environmental stimuli should start in the breeder's home and this is why it is better for them to be raised in domestic circumstances rather than in a barn, shed or kennel. Every effort should be made to systematically introduce a broad range of experience, which you should continue at and away from home and you should include frequent experience of both rural and urban areas. It is important that all experience should start where your puppy is relaxed and with less challenging situations and gradually build up.

Could our dog become fearful?

Developing a dog's behavioural organisation from early puppyhood reduces the likelihood of it developing fearful behaviour in response to everyday experiences. Of course, fearful behaviour can still occur as a consequence of a severely frightening experience or repetitions of a less significant experience.

Should we reassure our dog when it is frightened?

No. Your dog will not understand words and physical comfort used in an attempt to reassure it and they may accidentally reward fear, increase the extent to which it is shown and the likelihood that it will reoccur. The best approach is to behave as if nothing has happened. Praise your dog if he does not show fear in circumstances in which apprehension might have been expected.

What are the likely effects of fear?

A dog may respond to what it is frightened of by moving away from it or behaving defensively, although other reactions, such as freezing and appeasement can also occur. The degree of reaction and the distance at which it occurs depends on the level of stimulation, the dog's sensitivity to it and what it has learned on previous occasions.

Defensive behaviour can become increasingly overt and the dog may look confident. This happens when a dog learns that the things it growls or barks at go away. On most occasions they would go away anyway, but to the dog it seems that they go away because of what it does.

What should we do if our dog's fear becomes more serious, persistent or defensive behaviour develops?

If you dog's fear is such that you feel that its welfare is compromised and/or it starts to use aggression as a way of coping, refer to 'Further help' page 20.

Vaccinations versus early behavioural organisation

Unfortunately, the period critical to a puppy's early development is also critical to the inoculation programme that protects it from Parvovirus, Hepatitis, Lepto-spirosis and Distemper. It is often suggested that during this time a puppy should not be allowed out of the house and garden, which is detrimental to behavioural organisation because of the consequent lack of experience.

Is there a compromise? Yes.

1. There are inoculation programmes that start and finish earlier than the traditional norm.

2. Discuss this with your veterinary surgeon before or as soon as you get your puppy. Programmes vary because some breeds are more susceptible than others and some areas can have a higher risk factor than others.

3. In addition to 1, carrying your puppy prior to the completion of the initial vaccination programme helps to reduce his exposure to sources of infection. Wrap him in a blanket so that if he does have a toileting 'accident' there is no need to put him down until you get home or back to your car.

For more information about the appropriate development of puppy behavioural organisation see 'How to Have a Happy Puppy', also published by The Pet Behaviour Centre.

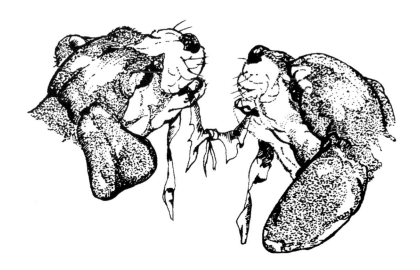

PROBLEMS RELATED TO PUPPY DEVELOPMENT

How to prevent chewing

Puppies need to chew, especially when their milk teeth are replaced by adult dentition. Puppies that get into the habit of chewing are sometimes difficult to stop, long after the need to chew has passed. The sensible course of action is to ensure that the areas a puppy is left in when unsupervised deny it the opportunity of inappropriate chewing. This ensures safety, such as in the case of electrical wiring, as well as avoiding damage to carpets, furnishings, etc. Providing a chew-free area can be difficult in the average household. Child-gates can be used to section off an area, various companies produce indoor kennels made of metal, and for smaller dogs and younger puppies types of playpen are available. These pieces of equipment are cheap in comparison to new kitchen cabinets, etc.

Leave your puppy with appropriate chew items (readily available in pet shops). Do not use old shoes, clothes, wood, and other items similar to things dogs are expected to leave untouched. Once the teething stage is over unsupervised access to other areas of the home can normally be allowed. The kennel/pen can be folded away and stored for use with your next puppy, kept as its bed, or resold.

If you catch your puppy in the process of chewing something you do not want him to, replace it with something appropriate and praise him for chewing it. Don't punish him (see 'Apprehension and defensive behaviour', 6, page 18), you are at fault for giving him the opportunity. Learn from experience and do not repeat the mistake.

Preventing inappropriate toileting

It is important to understand that toileting on a particular surface, eg. grass, is learned through association. Provide frequent opportunities for your puppy to relieve itself in the appropriate place, e.g., garden. Anticipate when he is likely to need to go such as after feeding and waking and take him to his toilet area. Do the same if you see him getting ready to go or catch him in the act. Provide newspaper by the door leading to the area you want him to use for toileting when you cannot supervise or in the indoor kennel/pen if you are using one.

Preventing play biting

In pack society puppies play physical games with each other and can pester adults by pulling ears, tails, etc. As they grow up, adults and littermates alike become increasingly intolerant of their sharp teeth. By 18 weeks of age puppies learn that mouthing or play biting can produce an unwanted response and to control the strength they use. When a puppy is introduced into the family, this process is normally incomplete. The family must take over where the puppy's mother and littermates left off.

How is this done?

Whenever the puppy uses its teeth in play the person concerned should respond with a 'NO', then ignore the puppy for a few moments. If the puppy seems to turn this into a game or to get attention, say nothing and freeze instead, making mouthing counter-productive. Alternative techniques for developing bite inhibition are normally taught at puppy socialisation classes. Whatever method is used, the outcome should be that the puppy learns:

1. To limit the strength of its bite in both play and for real.
2. That biting is counter-productive as an attention-seeking device.
3. To cope with frustration when it does not get something it wants.

The good behaviour guide

BOISTEROUSNESS AND GENERAL LACK OF CONTROL

How can we avoid our dog becoming boisterous?

Generally speaking, a dog becomes boisterous in response to the people and animals it interacts with. Conversely if everyone around him is calm he will learn to be calm. These rules should help:

RULES	BECAUSE
1. Do not shout at your dog in an attempt to control it.	Your dog may continue to be excited because he misinterprets this as your excitement. Additionally, he is rewarded by your attention. Any anxiety caused by shouting may compound the problem.
2. Ignore behaviour you don't want your dog to repeat.	Do this as much as possible because a response may reward with attention, making it more likely the behaviour will be repeated.
3. Do not punish your dog if he jumps up. 	Dogs will often lick the face of group members they wish to appease, for which, when the member is human, they have to jump up. The more aggressive you become the more your dog will have to jump up. If you ignore him, however, the behaviour should fade away over time (rules 1 and 2 also apply).
4. When you or visitors meet your dog, remain cool.	The more you initiate or respond to greeting behaviour the more exuberant your dog will become.
5. Follow these rules, including 3 and 4, even if your puppy is tiny.	However hard it may seem, it is much better to start as you mean to go on than correct your dog when he gets bigger for something you taught him to do.

6. Be prepared to temporarily segregate dogs from boisterous children, when the children are active.

Boisterous children can adversely affect a dog's behaviour. A segregation facility, such as the use of a child-gate, is beneficial.

7. Ensure that your dog has a balanced diet appropriate for his needs.

There is evidence that poorly balanced diets can affect behaviour. Although very rare, some dogs can have food related hyper-activity. Your veterinary surgeon will be able to advise you on appropriate diets.

8. Follow the advice in 'Maintaining a good level of control' below.

How can we maintain a good level of control?

The main things to remember are:

a. Do not expect your dog to do something you have not taught it. For example, if you want him to lie down quietly when you have visitors you must first train him to do it. Start in ideal conditions when there are minimal distractions, e.g., when visitors are absent.

b. Be aware that dogs do not know the meaning of words. Words are just signals they learn to respond to. So don't get frustrated when you dog does not understand a signal it has not been taught.

c. Don't repeat signals, your dog may learn to ignore them. If your dog is not responding go back to (a).

d. When your dog responds, reward him. The production of a titbit or toy in addition to praise will increase the chance of response to your next signal.

e. Do not use punishment when your dog does not respond. This will vent your frustration but will be detrimental to his learning and welfare. If your dog is not responding go back to (a). (Also see page 17).

f. Reward good behaviour your dog offers without being asked. Don't take him for granted, e.g., reward him if he chooses to lie down when you have visitors to encourage him to repeat it on future occasions.

g. Everyone your dog knows should use the same signals.

h. If you need to learn how to control your dog, i.e. to use sit, heel, come, down, stay, and retrieve, training lessons are essential. Your veterinary surgeon should be able to recommend a trainer or dog-training club near you. If not, shop around. There are good and bad training clubs and good and bad trainers. Ask to observe a class before attending with your dog. Look out for:
Kind and effective training techniques using rewards not punishment.
Trainers whose demands are compatible with your aspirations.
Classes that are not overcrowded.
Classes without aggressive dogs that may affect your dog's behaviour.

i. Sending dogs away for training is not recommended. Courses for both the dog and owner are ideal especially because the techniques used can be approved and practiced by the owner.

j. Clicker training is a highly effective and fun training technique. See 'Go Click' also published by The Pet Behaviour Centre.

k. A dog that has developed low social inhibition can be difficult to control. Follow the advice for preventing it on page 14.

SEPARATION PROBLEMS
What is separation anxiety?
There are a variety of reasons why problems occur when owners are away from home. In general terms symptoms, such as destruction, vocalisation, and toileting, may seem similar but they vary in detail. Causes include:

- *Fear of things outside or inside the home, or anxiety that they will reoccur.*
- *Redirected territorial behaviour.*
- *Continuance of nuisance attention-seeking behaviour.*
- *Learned behaviour.*
- *Over-activity/inappropriate play behaviour.*
- *Frustration (e.g., because the dog did not expect to be left behind).*
- *Over-attachment (separation anxiety).*

Separation anxiety occurs when a dog becomes anxious when separated from the owner due to over-attachment (hyper-attachment). The symptoms vary but can include:

(i) Destructiveness – as a result of trying to follow the owner, i.e., by biting/scratching at and around doors or windows in the direction by which they left.

(ii) Vocal behaviour of a type consistent with calling back the person they are over-attached to.

(iii) Loss of toilet control.

These are accompanied by:

(a) Shadowing the person they are hyper-attached to.
(b) Anxiety or depressed behaviour when the person prepares to leave.
(c) Excessive greeting behaviour.
(d) Wanting to be in physical contact with or near the person when they settle.
(e) Distress if separated from the person when they are at home.

What can be done to reduce/prevent over-attachment?

RULES	BECAUSE
1. Do not respond to needy attention-seeking behaviour, licking, pawing, etc. Give affection on your initiative, when your dog is relaxed and does not seem to need you.	If your dog 'needs' attention it may be expressing mild feelings of anxiety. Responding may accidentally reward those feelings, making your dog more dependent and less able to cope when you are not there to respond. Conversely, rewarding independence will develop it.
2. If applicable share the duties of feeding, walking, etc., between family members.	To reduce reliance upon one person.
3. Train your dog to be able to sleep away from the bedroom and to be able to settle in another part of a room when you sit down.	To reduce the likelihood of your dog developing dependency upon constant contact.
4. Accustom your dog to being shut in another room some of the time when you are at home. If your dog shows signs of distress try using a child gate first, rather than a closed door.	Helps to reduce his dependency upon you and provides a level between togetherness and total separation.
5. Be very matter of fact about going out and coming home.	If your dog is anxious when it knows you are going to leave, fussing over it may reward and increase its emotional state, reducing its ability to settle. Fuss on returning home may highlight the contrast with your absence.
6. Provide appropriate items to chew before going out. For adult dogs remove them when you come home.	Helps to stimulate relaxation. Removing chew items when you are at home helps to retain their novelty value.

Other points

1. Do not punish your dog if he has done something you consider to be wrong while you were out. If you seem aggressive (even just harsh words) when you come home, your dog may become anxious in anticipation of your next arrival. When anxious he may bark, chew, or lose toilet control. In this way a vicious circle can develop. (See 'Apprehensive behaviour', 6, page 18).

2. Do not leave your dog for unreasonable periods of time. What is reasonable varies according to the facilities available – if in doubt ask your veterinary surgeon for advice.

AGGRESSION
Aggression related to resources
(other terms: status, dominance)

The dog fits in with family life because he and we are, in basic terms, co-operative hunters who live in small groups structured by what has been termed dominance and submission. What this describes is uninhibited and inhibited social behaviour.   Dogs do not have 'dominant' or 'submissive' personalities; their behaviour is affected by the outcome of interaction related to resources with other members of their group. For example, if a dog has something it values it will not give it up to another individual unless it is inhibited by them. A dog that can take it is less inhibited. The more uninhibited an individual becomes the more likely it will be to compete for resources and to become frustrated and agitated when its expectations are not met.

Dogs can become uninhibited if their owners give them a false impression of their ability to get resources, e.g., if family members always hand over some of their toast when their dog demands it. The more this perception develops the more likely the dog will be to use aggression to gain or keep access to resources it cares about. A lack of inhibition can lead to other problems, e.g., poor response to owners' wishes.

What should we do to help avoid our dog developing uninhibited social behaviour?

Control the things your dog cares about. You can deny access or use a 'when I say so', and 'earn it' approach, (e.g., earning by responding to your request to 'sit' or 'down', etc.). You can vary which you use according to what seems necessary, which is relative to your dog's attitude. Avoid using confrontational and aggressive gestures in an attempt to control resources because you are likely to cause fear and defensive behaviour. Unless a problem develops, for which you should seek further help, it is the essence of this approach that is important and whatever happens enjoy your pet, don't see your relationship as a 'dominance-submissive' struggle. The following are resources your dog may care about and why controlling it may help.

RESOURCE	REASONS FOR CONTROLLING
1. Food you are eating.	Inhibited individuals are more likely to give up food. Do not take your dog's food away when he is eating because he may become defensive – if not with you then with other members of the family. (See 'Apprehensive aggression'5, page 18).
2. Who eats first. You can feed your dog after you have had your meal if it tends to 'demand' to be fed.	When resources are low higher status pack members tend to eat first, so you may make a point.
3. Access to bedrooms and upstairs.	Regard these areas as your den.

4. Your dog's bed/favorite resting place.	You can displace him and occupy them yourself. Displacing him will let him know that you control his access.
5. Sitting on the furniture and your lap.	To many dogs these are valuable resources because of the comfort.
6. Toys.	If it seems appropriate you can control play and become the winner by the end of the game, keeping the toy until you start the next game. Dogs that lose are less likely to challenge over other issues.
7. Your attention.	Most dogs find owner attention highly rewarding.
8. Access through doorways.	Inhibited group members tend to give way.
9. Staying where he is causing you to step over or walk around him.	Asking him to move should have a similar effect to 8 above.

OTHER THINGS THAT MAY HELP	BECAUSE
1. Controlling pace and direction when on walks.	Changing pace and direction without warning, whether your dog is on or off the lead, means you literally lead the 'pack'.
2. Groom your dog daily. (Also necessary for good coat maintenance and to check for signs of ill health).	This reinforces status because he accepts the contact and if done correctly develops pleasant association with handling.
3. Do not let your dog mouth or bite you in play.	This teaches him to control the strength of his bite in real life, e.g., if he did compete for resources (see 'Play biting', page 7).

Dogs and children

Never leave dogs unattended with children. Dogs are predictable – if pushed too far over resources or are made to feel frightened they will react. Children are less predictable and can push dogs beyond reasonable limits of endurance. This, combined with a child's inability to recognise warning signals, can lead to disaster.

How can we do to prevent our dog becoming aggressive in territorial situations?

Good socialisation with people will reduce fear of visiting strangers. The advice for avoiding status-related problems will reduce the likelihood of your dog taking the initiative when people approach your home. (See page 14).

If your dog is aggressive in territorial situations, see Further Help on page 20.

RULES	BECAUSE
1. Do not encourage your juvenile dog to bark.	Barking develops naturally. If you encourage it, it can get out of control.
2. Do not shout at your dog to stop him from barking at people outside your home if asking him to be quiet does not work.	It may appear that you are barking as well and/or that the behaviour is rewarded by your attention.

3. Train your dog to perform another task once he has let you know someone is there, e.g., sit in his bed or go to another room, reward him when he does it.

Once your dog associates another action with the arrival of visitors he is less likely to become determined to guard the threshold.

4. Consider the option of shutting your dog away before people enter the house. Sit visitors in another room then bring him through to them. Alternatively, meet people away from home and walk home together.

Someone advancing over the threshold may cause defensive/territorial behaviour.
N.B. Recognition is often dependent on the dog's sense of smell rather than sight.

5. Give strangers a few small treats to give your dog or, if your dog prefers it, ask them to throw a toy a few times.

This teaches the dog that visitors are pleasant and therefore he is more likely to accept them and future visitors.

6. Delivery people, such as the postman and pedestrians passing the home, often trigger extreme territorial behaviour. Use good management to prevent accidents.

They are vulnerable because they go away when dogs bark, increasing their confidence to use aggression. Dogs don't understand that they have no intention to enter.

What causes defensive behaviour?

If a dog encounters something unfamiliar and unnerving or experiences an unpleasant event, it may move away or behave defensively. It can also learn to be defensive in anticipation of such events. (See page 4).

What should we do to help avoid causing apprehension and defensive behaviour?

1. The development of appropriate behavioural organisation reduces the potential for fearful behaviour (see pages 2 and 3).

2. Try to avoid situations where your dog may be attacked by another. Dogs that have been attacked often develop aggressive behaviour towards other dogs.

3. Do not leave children and dogs together unattended in order to avoid the dog being hurt and apprehensive in the future.

4. Never hit your dog by hand, with a rolled up newspaper, etc. Your dog should trust hands and people holding objects. Dogs do not hit each other; consequently it is an inappropriate form of reprimand.

5. If you have a puppy add more food to his bowl when he is eating. If your puppy learns to anticipate this he is unlikely to develop defense of food in later life.

6. Do not punish your dog, especially after he has done something and only interrupt him if you catch him in the act. Dogs have a 0.5 of a second in which to associate an action and its consequences. Telling him off may seem like unprovoked aggression, which may cause him to become defensive. (See 'He knows what he has done wrong, page 19).

But can we tell our dog off if he looks as if he knows what he has done wrong?

NO. The body language often interpreted as a look of guilt is actually submissive behaviour displayed in anticipation of the aggression, however mild, the owners normally use as punishment. An association can develop between the presence of damage/excreta, etc., and the owner's arrival, which triggers apprehensive behaviour even before the owner has seen what is wrong, but the dog cannot relate this to the act of causing the damage, toileting, etc. (See 'Separation anxiety', page 11).

How can we help avoid aggression between dogs in the same household?

When mixing dogs for the first time do so on neutral territory.

Follow the advice listed under status-related/dominance aggression, because improving the family's status will inhibit the dog's inclination to aggress towards each other. (See page 14).

Do not upset the status quo between the dogs. The least inhibited (dominant) dog should come first in everything it cares about and receive more attention than the subordinate, however much you want to mother the underdog because you feel sorry for it.

1. If possible, avoid having two dogs that are same sex, if they have to be the same sex, avoid similar age, size and type. Dogs that are similar are more likely to fight.

2. If you have two male dogs, discuss neutering the subordinate with your veterinary surgeon. This allows the status quo to be maintained more easily. Neutering both females will reduce the potential for aggression associated with the seasonal cycle.

Further Help

What can we do if problems occur even though we have followed these guidelines or if another type of problem occurs that is not mentioned here?

Consult your veterinary surgeon, who can ensure there is no medical cause. If appropriate you can be referred to a member of **The Association of Pet Behaviour Counsellors** who will be able to advise you.
Tel: 01386 751151   www.apbc.org.uk

Referred clients can see **David Appleby** at The Pet Behaviour Centre by appointment, or at one of the regional clinics he holds at the Queen's Veterinary School, University of Cambridge or at Veterinary Centres in Birmingham, Northampton, Nottingham, Derby and Wolverhampton and at the R.S.P.C.A. Leicester. Home visits are also available.

For details of clinics/home visits and talks/courses, contact 01386 750615 (main office), fax: 01386 750743 or visit www.petbehaviourcentre.com

How to Have a Happy Puppy and more booklets are available from your veterinary surgeon or from:

The Pet Behaviour Centre, Upper Street, Defford, Worcs, WR8 9AB

Price £2.75 + 75p p+p payable to Pet Behaviour Centre
info@petbehaviourcentre.com
www.petbehaviourcentre.com

Further Reading

"How to Have a Happy Puppy"

This booklet explains why and how the early life experience a puppy receives is so important to its temperamental development, clearly showing what steps breeders, potential owners and new owners should take to maximise a puppy's chance of developing a sound temperament.

"Aint Misbehavin"

Owning a dog can be hugely satisfying, and the more we can understand our pets, the more satisfying our relationship becomes. The dog's world is fascinating, and this 288 page book gives us a glimpse inside it which will usefully change our perspective on dogs forever. So often a dog is described as being 'naughty' when it is probably only displaying its natural behaviour - although in inappropriate circumstances. By understanding why dogs do what they do, we can often modify that behaviour to make them more suited to our social needs.

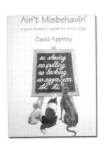

"Go Click"

This booklet is for those who just cannot wait to pick up a clicker and get going, but who are not sure where to start. It discusses the theory needed to progress through the initial stages of training.

NOTES